The Illustrated Address

and other tales

Collected and annotated by
Neil Stewart McLeod

With Illustrations by
Colin Bailey

The Illustrated Address To A Haggis

By the same author
A Ship in a Bottle
One For The Pot
The Clan Remembers
The Aching Heart
The Thorn Wi' Me
My Silver Box
When the Spirit Moves
A Cartload of Stories
The Persimmon Tree
Pure Whimsy
Songs and Poems of Frances McLeod

ISBN: 13: 978-1490984896

Dedication

To the memory of Colin Bailey and Gordon Baxter
and Scottish friends and clansfolk
who have let me entertain their company
with my renditions.

Foreword

by Gordon Baxter CBE, DL

Over the years much has been written about Scotland's national dish, Haggis, both fact and fiction, the latter usually in humorous vein. Much has been written.... and many jokes made at its expense. As a food manufacturer who believes that the proud marketing of my products is a top priority, I could say that nearly all the stories told promote haggis _ and bonnie Scotland - in a most unique and kindly way. Long may this free advertising continue!

Whenever.... and wherever....Scots are gathered round the world to remember St. Andrew their Patron Saint, or Rabbie Burns their national bard, the haggis has pride of place on the menu. A piper leads the way as the haggis is ceremoniously carried in to be placed in front of the host who 'Addresses the Haggis' in the words of the Bard, before plunging his skean dhu (his dirk) into it, spilling the contents - the aroma wafting around and tantalizing the taste buds of the waiting guests. The haggis is then served, well laced with the national drink of Scotland - true Scottish 'gravy', accompanied by mashed neeps (turnips) and champit tatties (potatoes). This ceremony, no matter how often repeated, will move the heart of the sternest Scot....and many have been seen to wipe a tear or two from the eye!

The haggis is, in fact, simply a super sausage or, as Burns describes it, the *'Great chieftain o' the puddin' (sausage) race'*, and like the sausage it was once common to many lands. Of course the contents must have varied as much as do those of the sausage in our own time. To such as still *'look doon wi' sneerin', scornfu' view on sic a dinner'*, I would point out that the most aesthetic of nations, the ancients Greeks, had a haggis of their own, which was immortalized by Aristophanes in 'The Clouds' around the year 400 B.C. Strepsiades entertains Socrates with a personal experience:

> Why, now the murder's out!
>
> So was I served with a stuffed sheep's paunch I broiled
>
> On Jove's day last, just such a scurvy trick;
>
> Because, forsooth, not dreaming of your thunder,

I never thought to give the rascal vent,

Bounce goes the bag, and covers me all over

With its rich contents of such varied sorts.

It's a pity we don't know what was 'intill't (in it). Where the ancient Romans are concerned we are luckier because a recipe has been preserved in the works Apicium Coelius. 'De Arte Conquinaria' (All about Cooking). The ingredients are chopped pork, suet egg yolks, pepper, lovage, **asa foetida**, ginger, rue, gravy and oil. The manner of stuffing, cooking and pricking is identical with the Scottish method of today even if the contents are quite different. Why everyone - except the Scots - stopped stuffing the paunch while they went on stuffing the intestines, the annals of gastronomy do not reveal. And why so many people furth of Scotland regard the haggis as an 'uncivilized' dish - and the sausage as a civilized one - is another mystery.

The choice of haggis as the supreme national dish of Scotland is very fitting. It is a testimony to the national gift of making the most of small means; for in the haggis, we have concocted from humble - even despised - ingredients, a veritable **plat de gourmets.** By tradition it contains a proportion of oatmeal, for centuries the national staple grain, whilst the savoury and wholesome blending of cereal with onion and suet is typically Scottish. Further, it is the thoroughly democratic dish, equally available and equally honoured in castle, farm and croft. Finally, the use of the paunch of the animal as the receptacle of the ingredients gives that touch of romantic barbarism so dear to the Scottish heart!

My recommendation to you, dear reader, is to taste and enjoy Scotland's delicacy....remembering always to spare a 'drap o' the cratur' for the gravy, before raising your glass.... filled with a Speyside Malt Whisky of course....in tribute to 'BONNIE SCOTLAND'.

With kindest regards

Sincerely

Gordon

GORDON BAXTER

GORDON BAXTER, C.B.E., D.L., L.L.D.
W.A. Baxter and Sons Limited
Fochabers, Scotland

Contents

Introduction

There are some very good reasons why this book needed to be written. Not the least of which, was the fact that so many people are interested to know the meaning of Robert Burns' famous and oft recited ode *'To A Haggis'*. My active involvement in the activities of the Scottish community led to my receiving many invitations to get up in front of an audience and brighten up the entertainment. Stories, singing and recitation were the arrows in my quiver. But it was not until I saw a performance by a true master of repartee, Tom Girvin, that I committed myself to the art of dismembering Scotland's greatest sausage. Since then, the occasions have been legion when wild thrusts and splattered napkins, have set the presenters rearing backwards and filled a dinner audience with mirth. My huge Highland dirk was christened 'Haggis Slayer', and with the help of Chef Ivan, at the famous 'Tam O'Shanter Restaurant' in Los Angeles, it has been used to disgorge the *"Warm, reeking,"* and *"rich..."* contents of as many as eighteen Haggai in a single Burns' Season. The popularity of the Haggis Ceremony, obligatory at Burns Nights, and derigeur at most Scottish banquets, is an ideal setting for airing out other poems on the subject of our national dish. So it was that people related additional tales to me, the best of which I have included here.

This book would never have come to publication had I not taken a locum in a Beverly Hills dental practice. It was shortly after graduating from the University of Southern California in1976. There I met, as a patient, Colin Bailey. He was a toy designer and illustrator who worked for the Mattel Corporation. Colin and I became great pals. I must credit him with the inspiration for the book.

He would dash off cartoons on every occasion; to celebrate a birthday, or explain what he thought of the stories I had told him while waiting for the anesthetic to work. My professional practice logo, Phil MaCavity, is Colin's creation. So are the wonderful drawings in this book. There is something just a little earthy about haggis, not to detract in any way from the gastronomical attributes of this excellent food. But, the perfection of dousing it with a dram, and the fluidity leant by hoisting a glass or two during the attitude adjustment hour which precedes most Scottish functions, does lend itself to the appreciation of a slightly naughty story. Nothing pleases the Scot more than to think that his neighbors south of the border are revolted by the idea of eating haggis. This probably accounts for the popularity of the flourish which is a part of its serving. Here are some stories about haggis. If they are going to offend you, or if you don't have the stomach for them, please close the book. Then forgive me and *'Turn a deaf ear, pretend I'm a friend'*. As for the rest, have a good time and enjoy a wee chuckle. It's good for the heart.

Neil Stewart McLeod

Phil MaCavity says "Just Floss 'Em"

Address To A Haggis - By Robert Burns

This poem was written by Robert Burns in 1786, shortly afer his arrival in Edinburgh. It first appeared in the Caledonian Mercury on December 20th., and in the Scots Magazine in January 1787. The text was included in the Edinburgh Edition of his poems. Oft recited and wondered at, here is an illustrated explanation of what the words mean.

Dr. McLeod was recognized for slaying Haggis at the Tam O' Shanter for over thirty years.

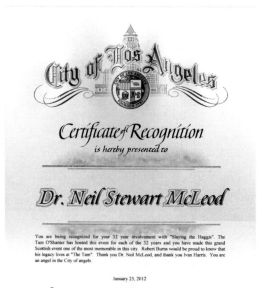

X

Address To A Haggis

By Robert Burns

Fair fa'[1] your honest, sonsie[2] face,

_____

[1]Greeting
[2]Jolly

Great chieftain o' the puddin-race!

Aboon them a' ye tak your place,

Painch[3], tripe[4], or thairm[5]:

---

[3]Paunch
[4]Tripe
[5]Small guts

Weel are ye wordy o' a grace

As lang's my arm.

The groaning trencher[6] there ye fill,

---

[6]Wooden Platter

Your hurdies[7] like a distant hill,

_____

[7]Buttocks

Your pin[8] wad help to mend a mill

In time o' need,

_____

[8]Skewer

While thro' your pores the dews distil

Like amber bead.

His knife see rustic Labour dight[9],

_____

[9]Wiped

An' cut you up wi' ready sleight[10],

Trenching your gushing entrails bright,

Like ony ditch

---

[10]Precise skill

And then, O what a glorious sight,

Warm-reekin, rich!

Then, horn[1] for horn, they stretch an' strive:

Deil tak the hindmost[2]! on they drive,

_____

[1]Spoons of curved horn (traditional)
[2]Slow ones

Till a' their weel-swall'd kytes[1] belyve[2],

Are bent lyke drums;

———————————

[1]Swollen stomachs
[2]By and by (in due course)

13

Then auld Guidman, maist like to rive[1],

"Bethankit!" 'hums.

Is there that owre his French ragout[1]

Or olio[2] that wad staw[3] a sow[4],

Or fricassee[5] wad mak her spew

    Wi' perfect sconner[6],

Looks down wi' sneering, scornfu' view

    On sic a dinner.

---

[1]Highly seasoned meat & vegetable stew
[2]Hotch potch, mixed anything
[3]Stall
[4]A fat pig
[5]Meat of small animals in sauce
[6]Loathing or disgust

Poor devil! see him ower his trash,

As feckless[1] as a wither'd rash[2],

His spindle-shank[3], a guid whip-lash,

His nieve[4] a nit[5];

---

[1]Pithless, feeble, wanting resource
[2]Rush
[3]Skinny arms and legs
[4]Fist
[5]Small nut

Thro' bloody flood or field to dash,

O how unfit!

But mark the Rustic, haggis-fed,

The trembling earth resounds his tread.

Clap in his walie nieve[1] a blade,

He'll mak it whissle;

An' legs an' arms, an' heads will sned[2],

Like taps[3] o' thrissle[4].

---

[1]Ample fist
[2]Cut off
[3]Tops
[4]Thistles

Ye Pow'rs wha mak mankind your care,

And dish them out their bill o' fare,

Auld Scotland wants nae skinking ware[1]

That jaups[2] in luggies[3];

---

[1]Thin stuff
[2]Splashes in bowls
[3]Wooden vessels with handles

19

But, if ye wish her gratefu' prayer,

Gie her a Haggis!

Horace

We often have Haggis in sunny Southern California. At Burns Nights, clan gatherings and Highland balls it is de rigueur. Some people like to add a little something after the *"Address to A Haggis"* by way of an explanation. From this has grown the custom of giving a rebuttal to the Burns' poem. You only had to hear *"Horace"* once to know that it was perfect for the part. Consequently it has been a part of the seasonal repartee for many years. When Terry Jones, of *Monty Python* fame, was asked if his poem could be printed in this book he said, "Yes, it sounds nice and quirky." Please send me a copy! So here it is.

Horace

Preamble:

by Neil McLeod

Some people ask me why I wear the tartan.

And what a Scotsman wears 'neath his kilt

Or "Tell me, what is it they call the Haggis?"

Och, their dreary remarks make me wilt.

I suppose I should worry about my answers

The way mother taught me to do.

And so it is that I beg all your pardons

As I tell you the tale young Horace went through.

Now 'fore I start let each one remember

My intention is not to offend

And if 'tween the lines

You take displeasure

Turn a deaf ear, pretend I'm a friend.

Horace

By Terry Jones

Much to his mom and dad's dismay

Horace ate himself one day

He didn't stop to say his grace

He just sat down and ate his face.

"We can't have this," his dad declared

"If that lad's ate he should be shared."

But even as he spoke he saw

Horace eating more and more.

First his legs...

...and then his thighs...

His arms, his nose, his hair, his eyes

Horace

"Stop him someone", mother cried

"Those eyeballs would be better fried."

But all too late for they were gone

And he had started on his dong.

"Oh foolish child," his father mourns

"You could have deep-fried that with prawns

Some parlsey and some tartar sauce."

But 'H' was on his second course.

His liver and his lights and lung,

His arms, his neck, his cheek , his tongue.

"To think I raised him from the cot

And now he's going to scoff the lot."

His mother cried, "What shall we do?"

"What's left won't even make a stew!"

And as she wept her son was seen

To eat his head, his heart , his spleen

And there he lay a boy no more,

Just a stomach on the floor.

Nonetheless since it was his they ate it.

That's what Haggis is!

Educating Willie

<u>REBUTTAL TO THE ADDRESS TO A HAGGIS</u>

tae A Haggis

Preamble

Well hello my friends and family

I have spoken here before

Of when Horace ate himself into

A Haggis on the floor.

And the chef who in a flurry

Slipped a Haggis from up high,

And he winced to see the damage

As the crowd laughed till they'd cry.

So not wanting to bore you all

I thought I'd try tonight

To tell the story of Wee Willie

When he finally saw the light.

Educating Willie

When Willie was a lad of six

He bit his finger nails.

He bit them at the table

Till he made his mother quail.

He sometimes chewed then till they bled

Right down to the quick.

He did it at a Tartan Ball

And made his mother sick.

Don't chew your finger nails Willie

His mourning mother would wail,

You'll turn into a Haggis

Like poor Horace in the tale.

That habit's hard to marshal,

Soon you'll do it in your sleep,

And chew away at pieces

That you really want to keep.

Then as she spoke the piper played,

And in marched to the sound

The chef and whiskey bearer,

They all paraded all round.

The Speaker started his address,

Wee Willie was surprised

When he saw him wipe his knife off

Right before his eyes.

Oh! Willie didn't realize

Och! Willie didn't ken

But he thinks he saw him murdering

The Haggis..once again.

He saw him stick the knife in,

He flinched when it went deep.

And the Haggis it just lay there

As if it were asleep.

Willie previously considered

Haggis was a sacred beast

That must be hunted on the hillsides

In the heather and the peat.

With a piper in the distance

Who will play in rueful setts

That will scare the little beasty

Round the hillside to the nets.

It's hard to catch a Haggis

Och! the art form's nearly dead,

You don't just shoot the animals

Or bash them on the head

You have to stalk them quietly

Not quite down wind from his tail

Cause their breath when they start squealing

Can cause your heart to fail.

But they're pretty furry creatures

And they keep themselves quite warm

In the coldest of the winters

Or the harshest Scottish storm.

And Highlanders for ever

Have cured and used the hide

To make the sort of Sporrans

That look rich and dignified.

Later Willie knelt at bedside,

Hands tightly wrapped in prayer,

And looking at his finger nails

He gave himself a scare.

"Dear Jesus, will you help me

Not to chew them any mare,

I don't want to be like Horace,

Just a haggis on the flair[1]."

---

[1]Flair - floor

When Willie went to bed that night

He'd brushed and flossed his teeth

And he tucked his fingers far away

Deep down beneath the sheet.

But soon he set to dreaming

Of the evening that had been,

And of how he saw them murdering

The haggis once again.

The horror struck poor Willie

Tears on his mother's face,

To see her laddie eat himself

Would just be a disgrace.

At school he told his class mates,

But they just laughed with scorn

And Willie in distraction

Chewed his fingers even more.

But he is starting now to wonder

If the rumor could be true

That the Haggis, like dear Santa,

Was just another story too.

The Tooth Fairy had vanished

For he knew that was his dad.

But this thing about the Haggis,

Well, it's really rather sad.

The Tartan Whatnot

John Findlay[1]

This is the tale

of Sandy MacSpartan

Whose pride and joy

was his fine kilt of tartan,

And to tell you the truth,

if as yet you don't know it,

Sandy MacSpartan

wore nothing below it.

1

We have tried at length to contact John Findlay, the author of this poem, and have been unable to discover his where abouts. A debt of thanks is owed to whomever it was for the hours of mirth this poem alone have brought to the Scottish community.

The lassies around would all hope for a breeze,

That would blow Sandy's kilt way up over his knees,

Then their eyes would sparkle, and look so forlorn,

When they gazed at what Sandy had, under his sporran.

At Burns night's dinners,

    he was always selected,

To carve up the Haggis,

    for the newly elected,

And one night as he stuck

    the knife in with a slap,

The whole bloody mess

    slipped into his lap.

He lifted his kilt to get rid of the dollop,

Six ladies in front hit the floor with a wallop,

Doctor Greig shouts, "They've fainted, as sure as you're born".

For they glimpsed at what Sandy had under his sporran.

His kilt was a mess with Haggis and stuff,

"Och! Don't let that worry you", cries Mrs. MacDuff,

"I'll wash it in water and soak it in lye,

And just spread it out on the heather to dry."

But to Sandy's despair,

    his kilt shrank such a lot,

That it didn't quite cover

    his highland whatnot,

The parson's wife said,

    "My! Is that Gabriel's horn?"

When she gazed at what Sandy had,

    under his sporran.

"If you can't keep that hidden, you might camouflage it."

Said English militia man, Captain Sam Paget,

So artist MacNab[1], who hailed from Dunbarton,

He painted the thing the same as his tartan.

---

[1]Some texts say "artist McRembrant"

Now all of you ladies who are looking for thrills,

Just go to Scotland and head for the hills,

For there in the glen, where Wallace once fought,

Is the one man on earth with a *tartan whatnot!*

The Fallen Haggis

Anonymous[1]

This poem was published in *TackTalk* Vol.8, #4 March 1984, the newsletter for the Royal Scottish Country Dance Society Teachers Association (Canada), under the title 'The Imagined Catastrophe'. Many attempts to discover the author have proved in vain.

Great Chieftain, it would appear

Ye've had some trouble getting here,

An' I've nae doot you're feeling sair,

Efter yer contact with the flair,

In which I fear ye cam' off worst,

A see one o' your ends is burst...

Although the poet said, "Fair fa',"

That wisnae what he meant at a',

And when upon the flair ye duntit

Yer 'chef", puir man, was fair affronted;

His face grew red as any beet

When ye gaed slithering tae his feet.

The Ha'keeper breathed a silent prayer,

An' thanked the Lord he'd swept the flair,

While Robbie, in his Ayrshire tomb,

Was nae doot birlin' roon' and roon'.

Ye cam' into that croodit ha',

Held aloft "Abane them a',"

Fu' o' steam an' Scottish pride,

Lookin' rich an' dignified,

An' then doon frae yer perch ye fell,

While all the audience laughed like ....

For sic'a superior kind o' puddin'

Yer doonfa' wis richt sair an' sudden,

An' noo ye lie here in disgrace,

Wi' shame upon yer "sonsie face,"

Dae ye expect me tae address

A Haggis that's in sic a mess?

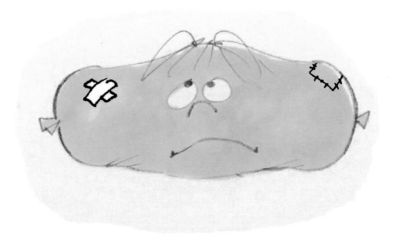

For slidin' off that groanin' trencher

Ye've mair need o' a vote o' censure.

Slaying the Haggis

Haggis is a simple Scottish dish elevated and revered because of Robert Burns' "Address to A Haggis" which draws attention to the honest truth of the equality of men and that even those raised on a humble diet may grow to be finer specimens than their fancier-fed counterparts. The ceremonial presentation of the Haggis should be rousing and simple, not gaudy and showy. It involves piping the dish in and around among the dinner guests and delivering it to a sturdy small table. The Haggis is usually borne in on a simple silver platter by the Chef who made it. A wooden platter would be better to enhance the realism of "the groaning trencher". The Haggis should be simply dressed with juniper or other wholesome greenery around it, but it should not be punctured with holly or covered with anything which would detract from its simple rude form.

Chef Ivan Harrison and Dr. Neil McLeod
At the Tam O' Shanter

A large skewer is a favorite addition which might be driven into the haggis at an angle ostensibly to stop it from rolling off the tray, but in reality to be drawn out with relish when the appropriate reference is made in the poem.

At the Athenaeum with Chef Kevin Isacsson and Piper John Mclean Allan

The piper should lead the parade, followed by the chef, holding the platter at eye level, his chin up and hat jauntily back. Following them, will be the speaker or speakers one of whom may bear the whiskey. They might be followed by standard bearers and men at arms. Depending upon the size of the gathering and the degree of ceremony required, there may be more than one piper and even a drummer, but certainly not a whole band. It is very important to remember that every one who stands up and takes part in the ceremony, should be comfortable with, and prepared to arm himself with a glass, and submit to the 'distasteful' habit of drinking a shot of whiskey. Considerable luster is added to the occasion if the distribution of the shots and the manner in which they are consumed is properly conducted. There is no point in expecting a pause between the end of the address and the distribution of the glasses to do more that kill the drama of the moment. Those glasses must be filled by the whiskey bearer as soon as he reaches the table while the piper is keeping the company occupied. Then, ready for the poem, the ceremonial entourage gathers round the table, grasp their glass and falls back into line. One solitary glassful with the bottle and a plain white napkin are all that remain beside the haggis. There is great room for embellishment here if a larger table is used. Pictures of the bard, and other memorabilia could be displayed off to the side. But my personal preference is for simplicity. It would make Rabbie "burl aroon in his Ayreshire tomb" to see what they are doing to the presentation of haggis today.

Fueled by the curiosity folk have for what on earth the words mean, and fanned by the appearance of humorous and irreverent texts, a rebuttal to the *Address To A Haggis* has become fashionable all over the United States. These stories, although slightly ribald, do strike notes of enchantment in the hearts of those who may have indulged during the attitude adjustment hour preceding the dinner. Not least amongst these, *Horace*, was composed by Terry Jones, of *Monty Python* fame. I have been reciting it for over thirty years. When I asked him if I might include it here, his response was that I may, and that it was a nice quirky idea, and could he have a copy!

So there you have it! It is best to keep the ceremony short and sweet. Parade it all in, recite the poem, hoist a glass and tell a funny story afterwards before parading away. During the last thirty three years I have slain the haggis at the Tam 'O Shanter Restaurant at least six times a night for a minimum of two nights every Burns Season. Ivan Harrison, the famous chef, participates with me, "bearing in the beast" which he prepares. He is a great sport and stoutly built, and allows me to identify him when I *"mark the rustic, haggis fed"*. I warrant that my dirk which I use to slay the haggis has been used over five hundred times for the purpose. That must be some kind of record.

Haggis Slayer

Pierced Trays

The art of redefining the contour of fine silver trays is one that is more particularly Scottish than perhaps, any other nationalities - a reputation that the great halls of silversmiths in London and Sheffield are prone to envy. Whether this skill blossomed from an innate sense of impecunity, or from the natural latent genius for which we are so proud, is left to conjecture. But the fact clearly remains that more pierced silver is to be found in Scotland, and in Scottish enclaves than any where else in the world. Why you might ask has this unusual specialization developed? Well the answer lies in the frequency with which the haggis is slain in late January each year.

Scotland is famous of course for her two principal exports, her brains, and the antidote, whisky. It is the fortification with the latter in preparation for the "Address To A Haggis", that is, in all likelihood, responsible for the abundance of perforated chargers. Armed with dirks, it is not uncommon for exuberance to foreshadow good judgment in the lavish swing that plunges the blade into the warm and reeking bladder, allowing the tip to score and skewer the entire table display through to the richly varnished table boards beneath. If the knife can be retrieved, the tray will need treatment with planishing hammers and silver solder before the buffing wheels on the lathes can retrieve its former luster.

Nor should you doubt any part of this report, for every word of it is as true as the light of day. Examination of old copies of the *'Daily Breeze'* from 1988 will reveal an account of a similar occurrence, when, before the Royal Scottish Country Dance Society, Tom Girvin, that well known radio personality, had difficulty removing his dirk from the haggis for exactly the same reason. Years later Tom's offer to have the tray repaired was declined in favor of its value as a memento of that valiant stab.

"No," you might say, this cannot be the case; such a fabrication, such whimsy is more than is creditable. Yet I can tell you with no exaggeration, that in 1997 I stood right beside Joseph McClure Swindle, who, suitably reinforced with fifteen year old Talisker, slew the haggis at the Castaways one Burns Night. Joseph spouted forth,

> "His knife see rustic labour dight,
> An' cut ye up we ready slight,"...

and as he did so, he rammed his huge dirk down through the haggis tray and all. Paul Dimond, the British Consul General, and his lady Carolyn, were there to witness the thrust, as were the gathered members and friends of the Los Angeles Burns Club. The stage was set, and what a night it was. Later, after the loyal toasts, the "Immortal Memory of Robert Burns" was given by Ann Dwyer who, to our amazement transformed herself into Ann, the serving maid at 'The Globe Inn'. Her performance transfixed us, as she related "from personal experience" her encounter with the poet who used to frequent the inn. Richard Nathan, the editor of "Mad Dogs" gave the toast to the lassies, in a highly controversial parallel between Shakespeare and Burns' view of the fairer sex. Ah! but the answer probably lies right there, that it is in an attempt to impress the "lassies O", that we get into these predicaments of masculine excessiveness in the first place.

If you live in the Los Angeles area you can see the Haggis slain in true style at Lawry's Tam O' Shanter Restaurant, on Los Feliz Boulevard, on or around January 25th when the ceremony of cutting up Chef Ivan's excellent Haggis is performed six times each night. There is always piping and Highland Dancing and saucy ladies singing Burns' songs.

Entertainers at the Tam O'Shanter Restaurant

Authentic Scottish Haggis
Betty MacLeod 1988

Ingredients
1 Sheep's pluck
1 Large stomach bag
½ lb. Fresh beef suet
1 large cup of breakfast oatmeal, toasted slowly in warm oven
2 or 3 large onions
Salt and pepper to taste
1 large cup of stock or gravy

Method
Clean the stomach bag thoroughly, wash first in cold water then plunge into boiling water and

scrape away inside of bag, soak overnight in cold salted water.

After soaking over night, put aside with rough side out.

Wash the small bag and pluck and place them in boiling water for one and a half hours (90 mins.) Then cut away the wind pipe and gristle.

Mince the heart and lights. Grate half of the liver, the other half is not required.

Mince the onions and suet, mix all the ingredients and season with salt and plenty of black pepper and a pinch of cayenne pepper.

Pour over this a sufficient amount of pluck bree or gravy to make the mixture soft.

Fill the stomach bag a little more than half with the mixture, it needs room to swell about five eighths full. Press out the air and sew the bag up securely. Place into a pot of fast boiling water, and prick it with a large needle or skewer when it first swells to prevent bursting. Boil slowly and steadily for three to four hours without lid adding more boiling water as required. Serve very hot with neeps and tatties and nips in the style preferred.

Utilize the above instructions with the small bag to make an extra portion.

Definitions

Pluck	Heart, lights and liver
Lights	Lungs, not used much nowadays
Neeps	Turnips
Tatties	Potatoes
Nips	Half shots of whisky
Bree	Stock from boiling the pluc

Haggis Pie

Courtesy of Baxters, Forchabers

The traditional way of serving haggis is piping hot, accompanied by 'bashed neeps and chappit tatties' - that is, mashed swede and creamed potatoes - and a small glass of whisky. But there is another way of serving this delicious traditional dish.

50g (2oz) mushrooms, wiped and chopped
1 onion, peeled and chopped
25g (1oz) butter
411g (14 ½ oz) Scottish Haggis
45 ml (3 tbsp) stock
2 carrots, peeled and grated
Mashed potatoes for topping
A little milk

Lightly fry mushrooms and onion in butter. Add to haggis and mix well, moistening with stock. Turn mixture into a pie dish and smooth over. Sprinkle over grated carrots, then top with mashed potato. Brush with a little milk and cook in a preheated oven, 200°C (400°F) or gas mark 6, for 30 to 40 minutes until potato is golden -brown.

(Serves 4-5)

Annabel - Haggis Recipes for Burns Night

Courtesy of Baxters, Forchabers

Haggis Stuffed Peppers

2 green peppers
4 oz (100g) Scottish Haggis, cooked
1 oz (25g) breadcrumbs
1 oz (25g) grated cheese
1 teaspoon chopped parsley
1 dessert spoon stock

Half the peppers lengthwise, remove all the seeds, blanch for 5 minutes in boiling water. Drain well. Mix together haggis, breadcrumbs, cheese and parsley, and moisen with stock. Fill pepper halves, and sprinkle with a little extra grated cheese and breadcrumbs mixed together, if desired. Bake in a preheated oven, 350°F (180°C) or mark 4 for 20 minutes. NOTE: this is a delicious filling for Stuffed Tomatoes.

Serves 4

Burns Night Chicken

Courtesy of Baxters, Forchabers

2.7 kg. (6lbs) chicken
411g (14 ½ oz) Scottish Haggis
1 onion (peeled and finely chopped)
25g (1oz) walnuts (chopped)
10ml (1 dessertspoon) chicken stock

Blend together haggis, onion, walnut and stock. Use to stuff back-end of the chicken. Roast in the oven 190°C, 375°F, Gas No. 5 for 2 ½ hours.

The Haggis Tree

A Scottish Country Dance

* Pastoral, 2 Couples, 32 bars   Devised by John Drewry

* Tune "Herr Roloff's Farewell", (J. Scott Skinner) - "Harp and Claymore"

BARS

1 - 4   First couple set, then, giving right hand cross over

5 - 8   First and second couples, set, then the ladies dance straight across to opposite side as 2nd man
         casts to the top on the men's side and 1st man casts off to second place on the ladies' side. (First
         couple are on the ladies' side amnd second couple on the men's side of the dance.)

9 -16   First and second couples set, then dance "La Baratte" with the opposite person to change sides.

17-24   First and second couples set, and dance right hands across onr and a quarter times round (four
         steps); first couple dance through original places and cast of to second place on won sides, as
         second couple turn with the right hand half way round dancing up to top place on own side.

25-32   Second and first couples set on the side, dance four hands round to the left half way round, they
         turn partners with both hands once round opening up to reform the circle, then they dance four
         hands round still to the left to return to their own sides.

REPEAT
         A "Pastoral" is danced to slow airs with slow Strathspey-like steps

Neaps An' Haggis

A Scottish Country Dance

*Reel, Two Couples, 32 Bars   Devised by John Drewry
*Tune - "The Barnyards of Dalgaty"

BARS

1 - 8   First couple dance a reel of three acorss the dance with 2nd man, 1st man dances across giving left shoulder to his partner, while 2nd man dances up into 1st man's place to start. 2nd man finishes in his own place facing out.

9 -10 1st man, giving right hand to 2nd lady, crosses her into place, while she goes straight across the dance into her partner's place.

11-12   First and second couples set facing diagonally in.

13-14   First and second couples advance diagonally inwards with two pas-de-basque. The men join hands with one another, and the ladies do likewise under the mens hands.

15-16   All continue setting on the spot. During bar 15, the men raise their hands, and, passing them over the ladies' heads, they lower them behind their backs. During bar 16 the ladies let go of hands, lower them, then raise them behind their partners' backs. It is not essential for the ladies to rejoin hands, they can just place them flat on the men's backs. (This is the Haggis*)

17-24　All circle to the left (sixteen slip steps) gradually increasing the size of the circle until it becomes and normal four hands round. All go round two and a quarter times so that first couple finish in second place on their own sides, and second couple finish in top place on opposite sides.

25-28　Second couple dance half a figure of eight round first couple who stand still.

29-32　First and second couples turn partners by the left hand.

REPEAT

*　　Obviously the common right-handed Haggis (Haggis Normalis), which lives mainly on Lilly leaves and neaps. It is quite distinct from the rare left-handed Haggis (Haggis Widdershinsia), which was last seen on the Witches' Step in Arran.

About The Author

Neil McLeod was born in Oxford in 1947, while his father attended Merton College. He was raised in Kenya in the 1950's, and received schooling from the Holy Ghost Fathers at Saint Mary's in Nairobi. The family returned to England before the flag was brought down and Kenya gained her Independence. Neil went up to Guy's Hospital to study dentistry and came to America as a Fulbright Scholar to continue his studies at the University of Southern California. Doctor McLeod is past winner of the Los Slamgeles Poetry Slam. He writes a blog spot called *"A Biting Chance"* where much more of his poetry may be read.

Doctor McLeod is a performing poet who has recited at Highland Games, consulate dinners and Burns Nights for the last 36 years. He is happily married, lives and works in Los Angeles, has three children, and practices as a dentist on Sunset Boulevard. His poem *"The First Thanksgiving"* is an increasingly popular seasonal favorite.

Contact Information
Web: http://www.drneilmcleod.com
e-mail: drneilmcleod@yahoo.com
Blog: abitingchance.blogspot.com

Dr. McLeod will willingly entertain requests to share his work with permission.

About the Artist

Colin Bailey was born April 11, 1926, in Shortstown, England. He was raised in Lachine, Canada and attended art school in Montreal. After serving with the Royal Air Force transport Command in World War II, he went to New York City and apprenticed with Peter Helck, the noted automobile illustrator. In 1949, Colin moved to the West Coast and worked for Russ Hart Studios as a humorist illustrator. In 1957, Colin became a freelance artist. His work won a variety of awards from the ' Illustrators' Club '. He had a passion for the sea, and built his own boat for his two sons who he dearly loved. He moved to Cambria in the Pines on the Central California Coast in 1982. His home there could easily be mistaken for an up-turned hull. His career continued by creating artwork for several firms including the Mattel Toy Company. Illustrations he drew of old mechanicals, planes and boats and trains, showed his meticulous attention to detail. He was a patient of the author for twenty five years, and drew the illustration of Phil McCavity which is the practice logo. He passed away after a nine year bout with prostate cancer and was be buried at sea. Colin was 75.

Ta Ta The Noo !

Other poetry books by Neil Stewart McLeod

A Ship in a Bottle - Poems by Neil Stewart McLeod Vol. 1.
Thirteen whimsical tales including the *Grosvenor's Tale* and *Ramming The Royal Yacht Britannia*. Neil McLeod draws on his life experiences, then, using his wit and gift with words, weaves a tapestry of images to bring those experiences to life for his readers.
ISBN: 9781490390840 (pbk)

One For The Pot - Poems by Neil Stewart McLeod Vol. 2
Twenty one highly original poems, including *Siafu, Chai* and *Mango*. Once you spread your wings in Africa there was no going back to the soft life. Dr. Neil McLeod, has deftly captured this unique, lost civilization, by sharing his unbounded childhood curiosity and joy, as only an accomplished bard might.
ISBN-13: 978-1489575104 (pbk)

A Cartload of Stories - Poems by Neil Stewart McLeod Vol. 3
Twenty stories told with simplicity and candor, including *"Petticoat Lane", "The Wristwatch of Flying Ace Mills"* and *"Losing His Wheels"*.
ISBN: -13:978-1490943022 (pbk)

The Persimmon Tree - Poems by Neil Stewart McLeod Vol. 4
Thirty poems about raising a family in California, including *"Three Bands of Gold", "Three Clocks"* and *"With Roger"*, not to mention doing battle with the varmints in the title story.
ISBN-13: 978-1491082362 (pbk)

The Clan Remembers - Poems by Neil Stewart McLeod Vol. 5
Fourteen poems that directly relate to the Hebridean Clan MacLeod, including *"The Song Of The Caurie Shells"*, *"A Lament for the Games At Coombs Ranch"*, *"It Takes Your Breath Away"* and the title poem which is an accumulation poem, a MacLeod version of the *"The House That Jack Built"*.
ISBN-13: 978-1490395371 (pbk)

Pure Whimsy - Poems by Neil Stewart McLeod Vol. 6
Includes *"Getting Back On Track"*, *"Grand Ma's Smile"*, and *"Vanishing Wisdom"* with over thirty other poems. Time and experience are captured through the author's lens.
ISBN-13: 978-1491082676 (pbk)

My Silver Box - Poems by Neil Stewart McLeod Vol. 10
Treasured memories that might not readily be told are g
ISBN-13: 978-1491083284 (pbk)

When the Spirit Moves - Poems by Neil Stewart McLeod Vol. 7
Twenty uplifting reminders of occasions when the human spirit is moved.
Includes "Mother's Hands", "The First Thanksgiving" and House of Sighs"
ISBN-13: 978-1491082737 (pbk)

The Aching Heart - Poems by Neil Stewart McLeod Vol. 8
ISBN-13: 978-1491082997 (pbk)

The Thorn Wi' Me - Poems by Neil Stewart McLeod Vol. 9
ISBN-13: 978-1491083109 (pbk)

Songs and Poems of Frances McLeod
More than a score original songs and poems, many with a lullaby quality, from the bygone colonial era; including *"Skye Lullaby"* and *"The Golden Wattle Song"*. Touchingly romantic haunting melodies.
ISBN-13: 978-1489580245 (pbk)

If The Ghillie Fits... Volume 2 of the dances of the Clan MacLeod, which, with *"Dances of and Island Clan"* form a definitive collection of MacLeod related Scottish Country Dances. These two books were co written with Ann Skipper, former Dance Mistress to the Clan MacLeod Societies. Each dance is accompanied by its story, dance notes, relevant music, and choreographic diagrams. 272pp. Available from author.
ISBN- 1-883267-00-5

Made in United States
North Haven, CT
13 January 2022

14720763R00051